AROUND — THE — WORLD

MINECRAFT MASTER BUILDER

Published in 2023 by Mortimer Children's
An Imprint of Welbeck Children's Limited,
part of the Welbeck Publishing Group
Offices in: London - 20 Mortimer Street, London W1T 3JW
& Sydney - 205 Commonwealth Street, Surry Hills 2010
www.welbeckpublishing.com

All information correct as of January 2023.

A CIP catalogue record for this book is available from the
British Library.

ISBN: 978 1 83935 269 0

FSC
www.fsc.org
MIX
Paper | Supporting
responsible forestry
FSC® C144853

Printed in Dongguan, China

1 3 5 7 9 10 8 6 4 2

Designed, written and packaged by: Dynamo Limited
Designer: Sam James
Editorial Manager: Joff Brown
Production: Melanie Robertson

The publishers would like to thank the following sources for their kind permission to
reproduce the pictures in this book.

Shutterstock: engel.ac 6T, 41BR; Marti Bug Catcher 6B, 40B, 57B; myphotobank.com.au
7; Lukas Gojda 8L; canadastock 8R, 56B; Joseph Sohm 9T; Sergii Figurnyi 9R; 4045 9B;
Tavarius 24L; Anthony Booker 24R; f11photo 25T; S.Borisov 25B; muratart 25R; Lauren
Orr 40T; superjoseph 41T; Tupungato; BL; shot4shot 56T; 360b 57T; ThanyathornP 57M.

Every effort has been made to acknowledge correctly and contact the source and/or
copyright holder of each picture any unintentional errors or omissions will be corrected in
future editions of this book.

AROUND THE WORLD

MINECRAFT MASTER BUILDER

Make real-life landmarks in Minecraft!

MORTIMER

CONTENTS

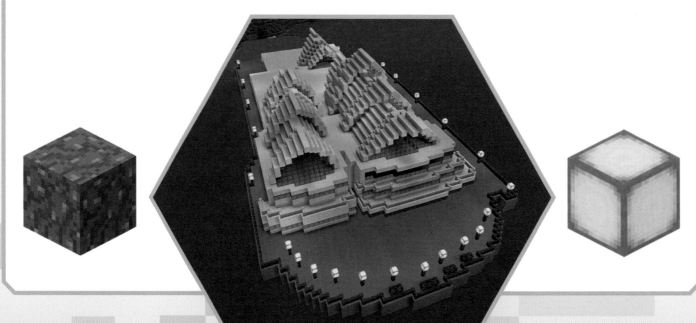

WELCOME TO AROUND THE WORLD: MINECRAFT MASTER BUILDER

Welcome to your go-to guide to building your way around the world. There are sculptures and statues, bridges and towers, castles and palaces, and so much more. Journey back in time across continents and cultures, and recreate some of the biggest feats achieved by humankind. This book is packed with step-by-steps and tips to help you on your way. So, let's get started!

NEW TO MINECRAFT?

If this is your first experience of Minecraft, then you're about to have a great time! Make sure you've got a solid grasp on how the game works and undestand the basic gameplay before you delve into the building. If you take the time to familiarize yourself with Minecraft, you'll be able to do far more when it's time to get creative. The sky's your limit!

EIFFEL TOWER
(Page 45)

TAJ MAHAL
(Page 72)

HOW MANY BLOCKS?

When you're building, keep an eye out for the symbols below. They will tell you how many blocks you need for each build.

Blocks

Slabs

DOING MORE

There's a great selection of builds for you to give a try in this book but why stop there? Once you've perfected your Minecraft skills using our step-by-steps, you can tackle any build you want. You can design your own palace, monument, bridge, skyscraper, or even blend them together. How about the Leaning Tower of Pisa on top of the Palace of Versailles? There is so much you can do!

STAYING SAFE ONLINE

Minecraft is one of the most popular games on the planet because it combines amazing building with fun. However, the most important part of the game is to stay safe when you are online.

Here are our tips for keeping safe:

- Tell a trusted adult what you're doing and ask before downloading anything.
- Speak to a trusted adult if you are worried about anything.
- Turn off chat.
- Find a child-friendly server.
- Only screenshare with real-life friends.
- Watch out for viruses and malware.
- Set a game-play time limit.

SYDNEY OPERA HOUSE
(Page 50)

TOWERS AND SKYSCRAPERS

From the ancient to the modern, all towers and skyscrapers have one thing in common—they're trying to reach the sky! Prepare to build up and up.

LEANING TOWER OF PISA

This world-famous tower in Pisa, Italy, is known for its dramatic lean to one side. It was begun in 1173 as a separate bell tower for the cathedral nearby. A few years later, before the third floor was completed, the building began to tip sideways. This was due to the soft soil it was built on, and its shallow foundations. Work continued, despite the lean, until the tower was completed in the mid-1300s. The tower now leans so sharply that it attracts visitors from all over the world.

BERLINER FERNSEHTURM

The Berlin TV Tower is the tallest building in Germany. The tower was completed in 1969 and is 1207 feet (368 meters) high. Mounting the ball at 656 feet (200 meters) was a challenge for the engineers. The supporting steel frame of the sphere had to be made on the ground, before segments were lifted up with cranes and then attached to the ring-shaped platform. The tower has over one million visitors every year.

CHRYSLER BUILDING

The Chrysler Building is a skyscraper in New York City, USA. It is the tallest brick building in the world. Completed in 1930, it measures 1,046 feet (319 meters). Walter P. Chrysler, who owned the building, asked for automobile icons to be part of the Art Deco decoration.

CANTON TOWER

The twisting design of this tower in Guangzhou, China, was based on a lighthouse near Odesa in the Ukraine. It was completed in time for the 2010 Asian Games. The tower is lit up by a colorful LED lighting system and is 1,954 feet (596 meters) tall.

BURJ KHALIFA

This skyscraper in Dubai, United Arab Emirates, is the tallest building ever built at 2,717 feet (828 meters). It has one of the fastest elevator systems, with a speed of 33 feet (10 meters) per second, traveling up 140 floors. The design of the tower is inspired by a desert flower called a spider lily.

LEANING TOWER OF PISA

Start with this iconic tower, although it's a little tricky with its famous tilt. Just don't let it fall over—its fate is in your hands!

MATERIALS

- QUARTZ BRICKS
- PILLAR QUARTZ
- LIGHT GRAY TERRACOTTA
- QUARTZ STAIRS
- CHISELED QUARTZ
- DOOR
- SKELETON HEADS
- ARMOR STAND
- IRON ARMOR
- IRON FENCE

STEP 1

Start by creating a circle base using **quartz bricks**.

x2

x7 →

STEP 2

Build up your base by 8 blocks—it will now be 9 blocks high.

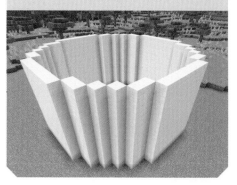

STEP 3

Fill in the top, so it's completely covered with bricks.

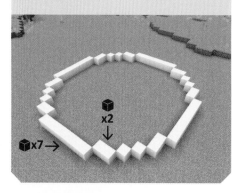

STEP 4

Create another circle around the top. Inset by 1 block (except at the front) on the left-hand side, and overlap by 1 block on the right-hand side.

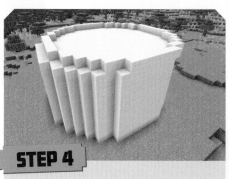

STEP 5

Build another layer 6 blocks high. Do this by insetting into the center by 2 blocks, as the picture shows.

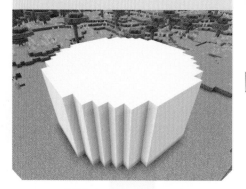

STEP 6

Add a layer of blocks on top, shifting everything to the right as per Step 4.

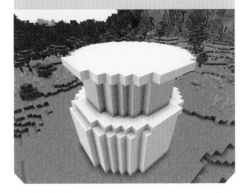

STEP 7

Using **pillar quartz** blocks, build up pillars around the outer edges. You should have 24 pillars in total.

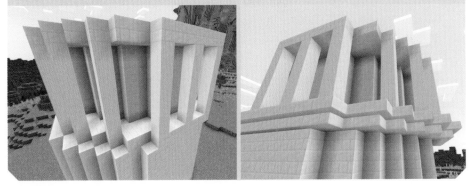

STEP 8

Add pillars along the bottom using **light gray terracotta** blocks that are 7 blocks high.

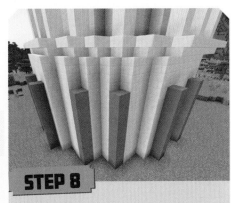

STEP 7

Add **chiseled quartz** on top of the **light gray terracotta** pillars. Then on each side, put upside-down **quartz stairs**.

STEP 11

Add some decoration and an **iron door** at the bottom of the tower where the flat edge is. We used a mix of **pillar quartz** and **chiseled quartz**.

STEP 12

Knock out a space 3 blocks wide and 3 blocks above the door. Place a **skeleton head** on either side and an **armor stand** with **iron armor** in the middle.

STEP 13

Repeat Steps 4-7 until your tower is 7 layers high.

STEP 14

This is how it should look with 7 layers.

STEP 15

At the top, build a smaller layer that is 3 blocks in from the left and 7 blocks high.

STEP 16

Add **iron fencing** around the top of each layer.

STEP 17

Knock out doors on the top layer where the wider sections are.

STEP 18

Knock out windows where the corners are.

STEP 19

Finish it off by adding upside-down **quartz stairs** to the top of the tower.

CHRYSLER BUILDING

It's the tallest brick building in the world and one of the prettiest skyscrapers around—can you rise to the challenge?

MATERIALS

- WHITE CONCRETE
- RED CONCRETE
- GRAY CONCRETE
- ANDESITE WALL
- ANDESITE STAIRS
- POLISHED ANDESITE
- BLACK TINTED GLASS PANES
- IRON DOORS
- IRON BARS

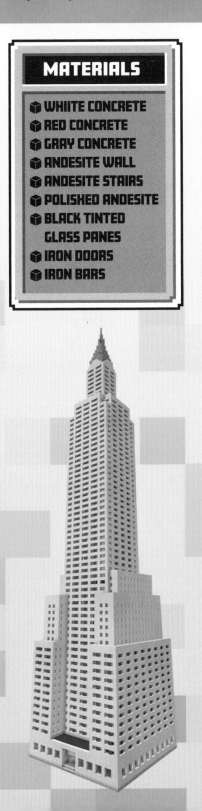

STEP 1

Use **white concrete** to make a 33 x 33 block square.

STEP 2

Fill in the square using **gray concrete** blocks.

STEP 3

On top of the square, add a frame in **white concrete** that is 5 blocks high with supports at each corner.

STEP 4

Use **white concrete** to fill the frame every 2 blocks along, leaving a space of 5 blocks in the middle. Place a **black tinted glass pane** in the middle.

x1 x1 x1 x1

x2 x2 x2 x2 x2 x5

Repeat on both sides.

STEP 5

Knock out the center base and replace with a line of **andesite stairs**. Add **iron doors** 2 spaces back with 1 space between them and fill in the wall above them with **white concrete**.

STEP 6

Make windows with 1 line of blocks above and below in the spaces. Use 4 **black tinted glass panes** to fill them in.

STEP 7

Repeat Step 6 and fill in windows and walls all the way around your building.

STEP 8

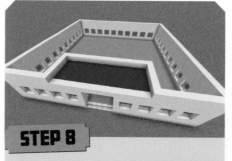

Build a border with **white concrete**; the doors and stairs will be in the middle. Make it 17 blocks wide and 6 blocks deep, and fill it with **red concrete**.

STEP 9

Alternate a pattern around the top of your build (follow the border from step 8 so you can still see the **red concrete**). Use a **black tinted glass pane**, then a **white concrete block**, another **black tinted glass pane** and then an **andesite wall** block.

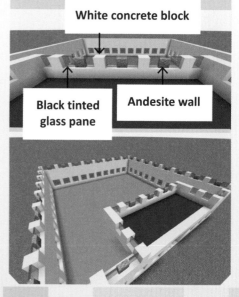

White concrete block

Black tinted glass pane

Andesite wall

STEP 10

Make your pattern from Step 9 into windows by adding a layer of **white concrete** along the top.

STEP 11

Repeat Steps 9 and 10 until you have 12 layers of windows.

STEP 13

On top of the back, left, and right sides of the frame from step 12, put 2 blocks of **white concrete** at each corner and then alternate between **black tinted glass panes** and **white concrete** blocks. On top of this, add a layer of **white concrete**. Do not build on the front of the building for the moment.

STEP 12

Starting from the front, inside the top of your building, build an inner frame 1 block back with **white concrete**, and then fill the gap with **red concrete**.

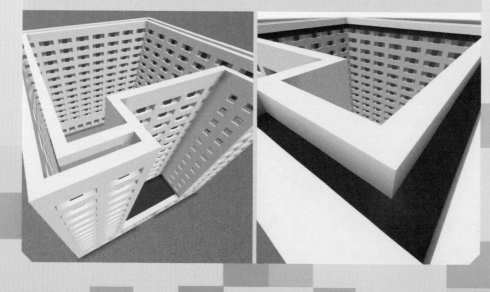

STEP 14

For the front of the building, use the alternating pattern from Step 9.

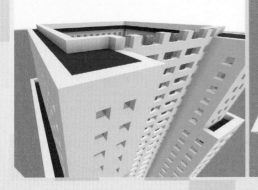

STEP 15

Repeat Step 9 on the front of the building until you have 7 more layers of windows. Repeat Step 13 on the other sides until they're the same height as the front.

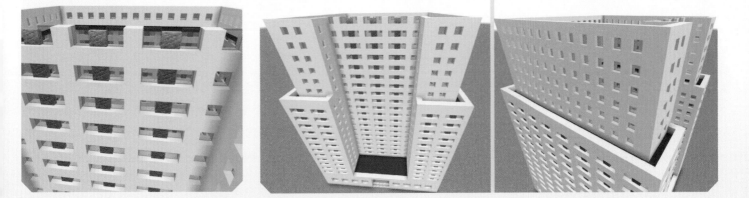

STEP 16

Build another inner frame of **white concrete** to fill with **red concrete**. Give it 2 blocks of space at the front and 1 block from the side.

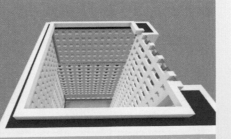

STEP 17

Build up 3 more layers of windows all the way around, using the same pattern as in Step 9 and Step 13.

STEP 18

Add another layer of windows. The left and right walls should now follow the indented center. This will create a frame for the left and right sides which can then be filled with **red concrete**.

STEP 19

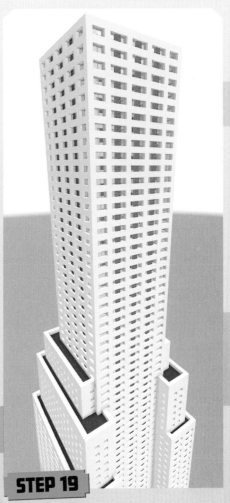

Continue to add 30 layers of windows using the alternating pattern from Step 9 all the way around your building.

STEP 20

Now create indents at each corner that are 5 x 5 blocks in size. The outer edge should be 2 blocks of **white concrete**. Place **red concrete** in the middle 2 x 2 blocks across in a square. Then indent a further 1 **white concrete** block back and use **black tinted glass** on the inner 2 corners. Alternate the pattern from Step 9 around the rest of edging and add a layer of **white concrete** across the top.

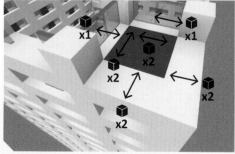

STEP 21

Add another set of windows and a layer of **white concrete**.

STEP 22

Create an idented frame all the way around the build and fill with **red concrete**. Add a 3-block-high wall with 2 central windows in each side.

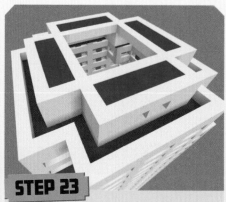

STEP 23

Using **white concrete**, square off the center, then fill the sides in with **red concrete**.

STEP 24

Build up from the top of the central square using the pattern from Step 9 and then add a layer of **white concrete**.

STEP 25

Add 8 more layers of windows and then a 4-block-high ridged edge.

STEP 26

Make sure each side looks the same.

STEP 27

On each side, use **polished andesite** 7 blocks across for 2 layers, then 5 blocks and then 3 blocks.

STEP 28

Build up so your **polished andesite** is 4 blocks high from every point.

STEP 29

Inside the **polished andesite**, create a cube at the top that is 5 x 5 blocks across. Knock the top corners out, making it 3 blocks across the top.

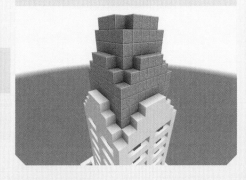

STEP 30

Keep building up and making the spire thinner, indenting the blocks as shown below. When you reach the point of your spire being 1 block wide, add 6 blocks of **andesite wall** and then top it off with 6 blocks of **iron bars**.

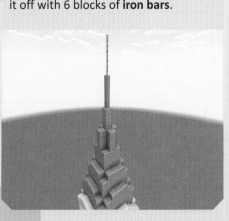

BURJ KHALIFA

Can you make the world's tallest building? It's going to go high!
Get ready to flex those building skills and reach for the sky.

MATERIALS

- WHITE CONCRETE
- GRAY CONCRETE
- LIGHT BLUE STAINED GLASS
- STONE
- STONE FENCE

STEP 1

Use **white concrete** to start the foundation. Step 3 has the measurements you'll need.

Raised block

x7

STEP 2

Build the top part of the foundation, referring again to Step 3 to help you.

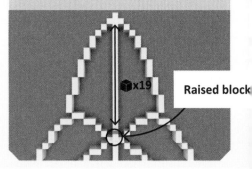

x19

Raised block

STEP 3

The foundation shape should look like this. These kinds of organic shapes are hard to create in Minecraft, so it may take a while.

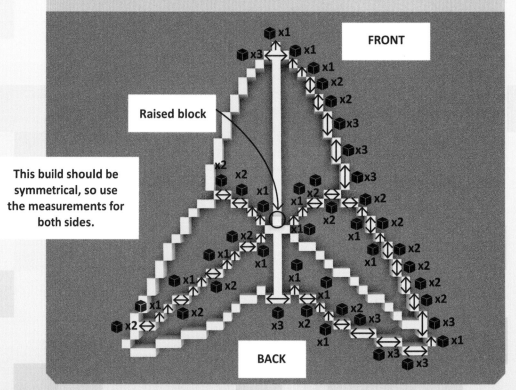

FRONT

Raised block

This build should be symmetrical, so use the measurements for both sides.

BACK

STEP 4

Add these rounded shapes to the back and sides of your foundation shape. Step 5 can help you with the exact positions.

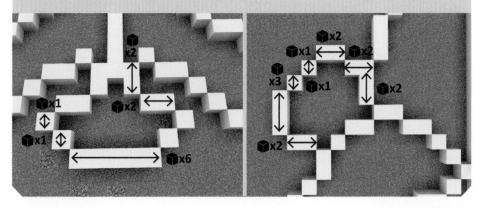

STEP 5

This is how your shape should now be looking.

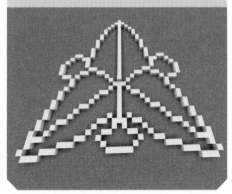

STEP 6

Add a layer of **light blue stained glass** to the top edges of your build.

STEP 7

Now add a layer of **white concrete** on top of your **light blue stained glass**.

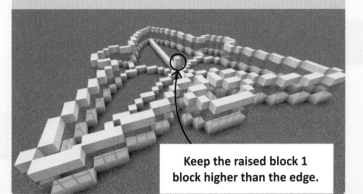

Keep the raised block 1 block higher than the edge.

STEP 8

Fill in the top of the rounded shapes you built in Steps 4 and 5.

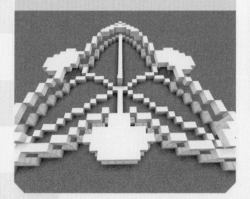

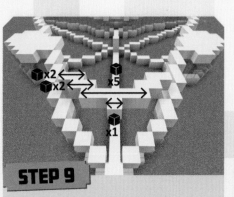

STEP 9

Build across the front middle using this as a guide. It starts 7 blocks back. Then, using this as your new front, add 2 blocks around the edges.

STEP 10

Fill in between the new front and the old front so it looks like below.

STEP 11

Add a layer of **white concrete,** then a layer of **light blue stained glass** and then another layer of **white concrete** to your middle shape.

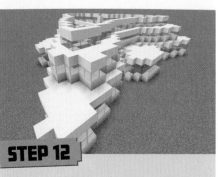

STEP 12

Indenting 1 block in from the middle shape, add a layer of **light blue stained glass** and then another layer of **white concrete.**

STEP 13

Bring the inner center line and raised block from the original shape up to this height too.

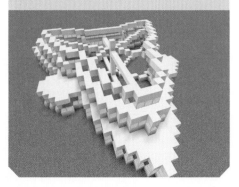

STEP 14

Indent by 1 block again and add a layer of **light blue stained glass** and another layer of **white concrete.**

STEP 15

Add layers of **light blue stained glass** and **white concrete,** and then repeat, so you end up with 4 more layers.

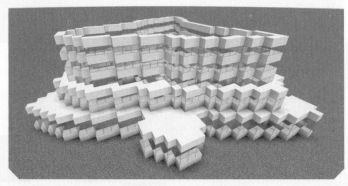

STEP 16

Add a layer of **gray concrete** to the top layer of your build.

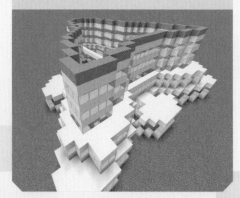

STEP 17

Add a layer of **white concrete,** but start it 6 blocks back from the front point.

STEP 18

Fill in front space with **white concrete.**

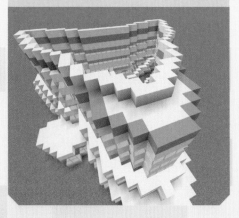

STEP 19

Add 4 more stacked layers of altenating **light blue stained glass** and **white concrete**.

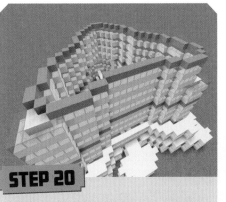

STEP 20

Add layers of **light blue stained glass** and **gray concrete**. Leave the left back corner free.

STEP 21

Build up 1 more layer of **gray concrete**. Then add 4 more layers of alternating **light blue stained glass** and **white concrete**.

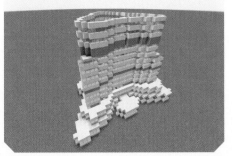

STEP 22

Indent from the front by 2 blocks with a curved shape. Add a layer of **light blue stained glass** and **white concrete**.

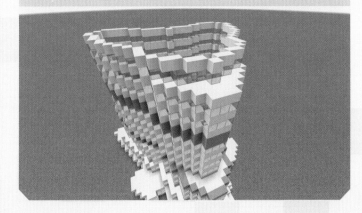

STEP 23

Add 4 more alternating layers of **light blue stained glass** and **white concrete**.

STEP 24

Add 1 more layer of **light blue stained glass**, leaving the left-hand corner ledge free.

STEP 25

Add a layer of **white concrete** on top.

STEP 26

Add a layer 2 blocks in height of **gray concrete**.

TOWERS AND SKYSCRAPERS

DIFFICULTY:
MASTER

BUILD TIME:
6+ HOURS

STEP 27

Add a layer of **white concrete**, and then check that your build is the shape below when you look down at it.

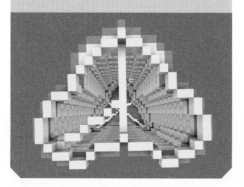

STEP 28

Add 12 more layers of alternating **light blue stained glass** and **white concrete**, leaving the right-hand corner ledge free. Repeat with another 12 layers and leave the left-hand corner space free. Then add a layer of **gray concrete.**

STEP 29

Add a layer of **light blue stained glass** and a layer of **white concrete**.

STEP 30

Add 4 layers, alternating between **light blue stained glass** and **white concrete**. Then indent from the front and build up 2 layers with **light blue stained glass** and **white concrete**.

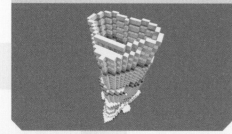

STEP 31

Add 4 more alternating layers of **light blue stained glass** and **white concrete**. Then add another open ledge on the right-hand side. Build up with 2 layers of **light blue stained glass** and **white concrete**.

STEP 32

Build up with 6 layers of alternating **light blue stained glass** and **white concrete**.

STEP 33

Leave a ledge in the left-hand corner, then add a layer of **light blue stained glass**.

STEP 34

Add 4 layers of alternating **light blue stained glass** and **white concrete**. Leave another right-hand ledge at the top.

STEP 35

Add a layer of **light blue stained glass**, then add a left-hand ledge. On top of this, add a layer of **light blue stained glass**, a layer of **white concrete**, and another layer of **light blue stained glass.**

STEP 36

Add layers of **light blue stained glass**, **white concrete**, and **light blue stained glass.** Then indent 1 block in and add layers of **white concrete**, **light blue stained glass**, and **white concrete**.

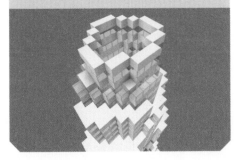

STEP 37

Add an open ledge on the right and then layers of **light blue stained glass** and **white concrete**.

STEP 38

Use 2 blocks of **gray concrete** over the top, and then build up 4 more blocks following the shape below.

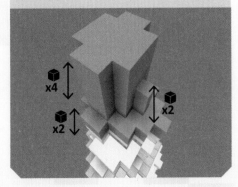

STEP 39

Go up another 4 blocks using the shape above as a guide.

STEP 40

Add thinner layers, use the final image as a reference. In the end, the **gray concrete** should be around 20 blocks high.

STEP 41

At the very top, add a single layer of **gray concrete**, 2 blocks high. Then add 4 blocks of **stone**. Finally, add 5 layers of **stone fence**.

SCULPTURES AND STATUES

From life-size to gigantic, there are many different sculptures and statues of the human form. All three-dimensional, they can be made out of many materials.

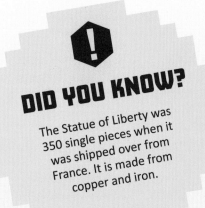

STATUE OF LIBERTY

This statue of a female figure represents Libertas (Latin for liberty), the Roman goddess of freedom. This huge sculpture was a gift from France to the USA. On her stone tablet is carved July 4, 1776—the date when America became independent from Britain. She has stood in New York Harbor, welcoming people to the city, since 1886.

! DID YOU KNOW?

The Statue of Liberty was 350 single pieces when it was shipped over from France. It is made from copper and iron.

EASTER ISLAND HEADS

Famous for its giant stone figures called moai, Easter Island—known as Rapa Nui to the people living there—is a small island in the Pacific Ocean 2,300 miles (3,700 km) west of Chile. Hundreds of stone statues were carved out of volcanic rock by the first Polynesian settlers beginning roughly in the year 1200. These sacred sculptures were placed along the coast, facing inland.

MOUNT RUSHMORE

This huge monument in South Dakota, USA, features the four heads of American presidents George Washington, Thomas Jefferson, Theodore Roosevelt, and Abraham Lincoln. Up to 60 feet (18 meters), their heads were carved into a granite cliff.

LINCOLN STATUE

Inside the Lincoln Memorial building sits the statue of Abraham Lincoln, the 16th president of the United States. The statue, carved from Tennessee marble, is 19 feet (5.8 meters) tall from head to foot—if Lincoln were standing, he would be US: 28 feet (9.5 meters) tall.

It took four days and 40 men to move the statue a couple of streets from Michelangelo's workshop in Florence, Italy.

STATUE OF DAVID

This statue of the biblical character David was created in the early 1500s. The sculptor Michelangelo began the work when he was just 26 years old. It is carved from a single block of marble and measures nearly 17 feet (over 5 meters) high.

DIFFICULTY:
EASY

BUILD TIME:
2+ HOURS

EASTER ISLAND HEADS

Are you ready to build your own moai? The original versions would have massive torsos buried underground, but all you can see are the heads!

STEP 1

Make a circle base, using **stone blocks**, at the bottom of your statue.

STEP 2

Make it 4 blocks high by adding 3 blocks up from your base.

STEP 3

Create the curved shoulders from the middle of the circle.

STEP 4

Fill out from the shoulder frames at the front, so the blocks step down.

STEP 5

Now add a circle to the top. This one has more straight edges.
We have made this circle white so it is clear, but in the second picture, you can see how it should look. This circle will be the bottom of the face.

STEP 7

Now fill in the front so the blocks join together.

STEP 8

Build up 5 blocks high from the back to the middle.

STEP 6

Fill in the back so the blocks meet the top of the circle.

STEP 9

Fill in the front 2 blocks high, but inset 1 block in.

STEP 10

Repeat Step 9, but inset 1 block in again.

STEP 11

Add a layer to the top that is 2 blocks high with 2 blocks sticking out at the front. This creates the sloping forehead.

STEP 12

Build a layer on the top that is 1 block high and inset by 1 block to form the top of the head.

STEP 13

Fill in the gap shown to form the bottom of the chin.

SCULPTURES AND STATUES

STEP 14

This is how the statue should look from a distance.

STEP 15

Use blocks down the side to create ears—make sure you do it on both sides!

STEP 16

Place blocks down the center and then in the middle in a "t" shape to form the start of the nose.

STEP 17

Add another layer of blocks at the bottom of the nose to finish it off.

STEP 18

Add a layer of **stone slabs** under the nose and 6 sets of upside-down **stone stairs** for the top lip.

STEP 19

Finish the lips by adding another 6 sets of **stone stairs** below the top lip.

The largest moai ever to be carved is called El Gigante. It is 72 feet (21.6 meters) tall and is still standing.

STATUE OF LIBERTY

Representing freedom, the Statue of Liberty is an iconic welcoming figure. Where will you put her to greet people?

MATERIALS

- OXIDIZED COPPER
- OXIDIZED COPPER SLABS
- OXIDIZED COPPER SLABS
- SMOOTH STONE

STEP 1

First you'll need to find or build an island like below for your Liberty Island.

STEP 2

Using **smooth stone,** build a stand for your statue that is 10 blocks high and 21 x 21 blocks wide.

STEP 3

On top of this, add a 2-block layer of **oxidized copper** indented in by 2 blocks on each side.

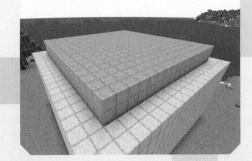

SCULPTURES AND STATUES

STEP 4

Add in 2 more layers of **oxidized copper**—indent each layer 1 in from the edges, creating steps.

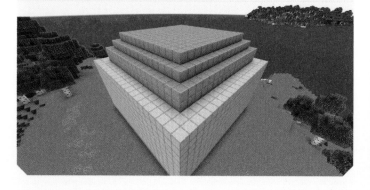

STEP 5

On top of the third layer, build a frame out of **oxidized copper** that is 8 blocks high.

STEP 6

On top of the frame build a second frame, 10 blocks high, indented in by 1 block.

STEP 7

Build a third frame 11 blocks high, again indented in by 1 block.

STEP 8

To create the statue's head, mark the center using 2 blocks in the middle of the frame. Build the frame for your head on top of the center block. This should be 5 x 5 blocks.

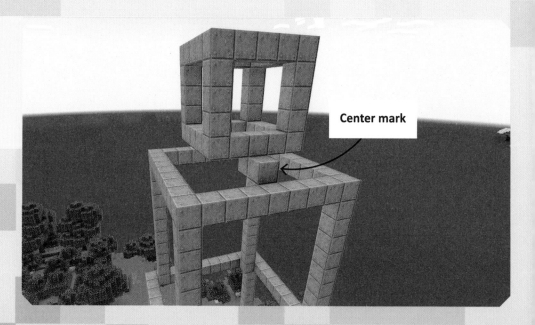

Center mark

STEP 9

Build the upraised arm on the right, like the picture below. It should go up in steps and be 15 blocks high.

STEP 10

Now build the arm that holds the tablet on the other side, close to the body. It should go down 10 blocks, with some steps and then out 8 blocks and in 1 block.

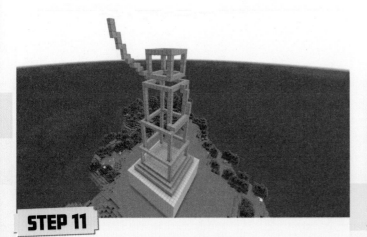

STEP 11

This is how your statue should look now.

STEP 12

Fill in the frames you made for the body and the head.

STEP 13

Fill out the arms so they're 3 blocks wide and 2 blocks high.

STEP 14

Add and remove layers of blocks across the body to create a draped look for the dress.

SCULPTURES AND STATUES

STEP 15

Add a foot poking out of the bottom of the statue.

STEP 16

Build the tablet onto the left arm – it should step up 3 times like below.

STEP 17

Knock out a series of blocks in the center for eyes. Add a layers of **oxidized copper slabs** to line the gaps. Then add a layer of **oxidized copper stairs** for the nose.

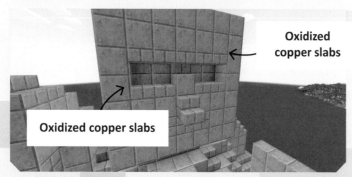

Oxidized copper slabs

Oxidized copper slabs

STEP 18

Knock out some blocks from the edges of the head to define the shape of the face a bit more. Add in some **oxidized copper slabs** for the mouth.

STEP 19

Now add blocks and slabs from the head to make the crown.

STEP 20

In the upraised hand, build the base of the torch.

STEP 22

Add some **smooth stone** ledges to the base.

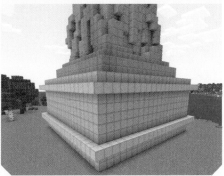

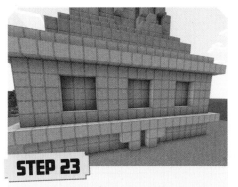

STEP 23

Knock out some blocks in the base and add a pattern along the bottom to create a grander-looking stand.

STEP 21

Add blocks around the edge of the torch and then build up the flames.

LINCOLN STATUE

Abraham Lincoln is regarded as one of the greatest US presidents of all time—can you do him justice? No pressure!

MATERIALS

- SMOOTH QUARTZ
- SMOOTH QUARTZ STAIRS
- SMOOTH QUARTZ SLABS

We've used light gray concrete to create a stage for our statue.

STEP 1

Start by making a base using **smooth quartz**, around 46 blocks wide by 50 blocks long.

STEP 2

Add a 10-block layer indented 1 block in from the base.

STEP 3

Build a ledge, around 30 blocks wide and 1 block deep, at the front onto both the base and the main block.

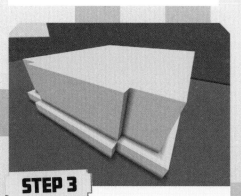

STEP 4

Make a square with a semi-circle (like a mushroom) on top. This will be the base of your chair.

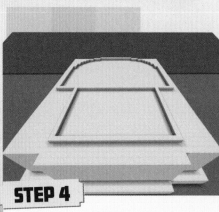

STEP 5

Fill the outline in.

STEP 6

Create an outline on the semi-circle and indent it from the edge as shown below.

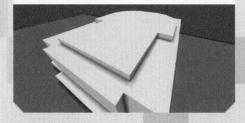

STEP 7

Create 2 oblong structures for the front of the chair's frame and then 8 supporting pieces for the back. It should be about 30 blocks high. Use blocks to outline the top.

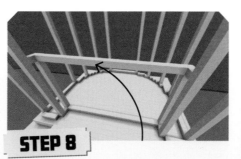

STEP 8

Put a line where the top of the seat will go, adding supports on each side to give it more structure.

STEP 9

Create an indented shape on the inside of the frame, ready to connect with the inner supporting pieces.

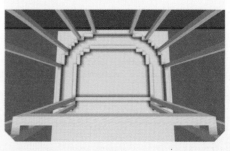

STEP 10

Build the rest of the frame, as seen below, and put in the seat. Then fill it in.

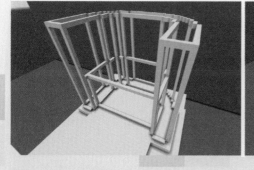

STEP 11

Start the statue by making the feet. Place blocks in front of the chair.

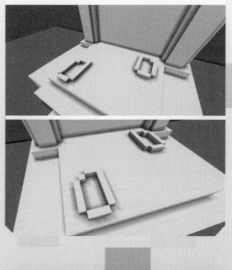

STEP 13

Build lines for the legs up to the seat—the one further away will need stair-like blocks, and the one closer will be more straight with a few steps.

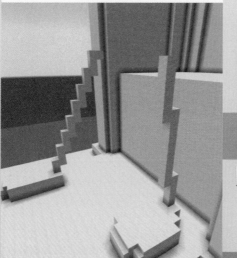

STEP 12

Put another layer of blocks on the feet, and then indent into the front and add one more layer.

STEP 14

Create the shape to form the rest of the legs, the hips, and the spine, and join it to the legs you've already done. The spine should be about 50 blocks high.

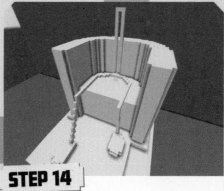

SCULPTURES AND STATUES

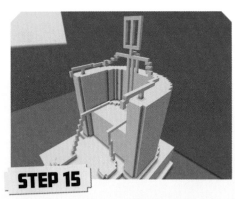

STEP 16

Build up 2 blocks high in a cross-like shape from the end of both the feet, to form the ankles.

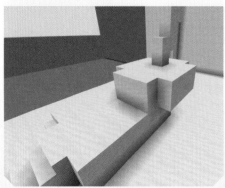

STEP 15

Make the shoulders and arms, running around the top of the chair. Make the head as shown, about 20 blocks high. Give the spine extra support at the back.

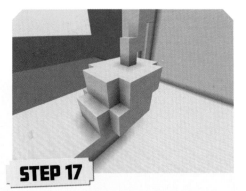

STEP 17

For the right leg, repeat Step 16 and indent by 1 block to create a step. Continue to add blocks all the way up the leg to the top.

STEP 19

Create this open space, 3 blocks down, at the top of the left leg where the knee would be.

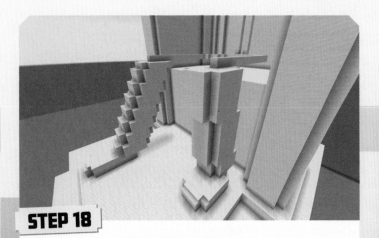

STEP 18

Now fill in the second leg by adding blocks over the ankle. Halfway up, bring them 1 block over again.

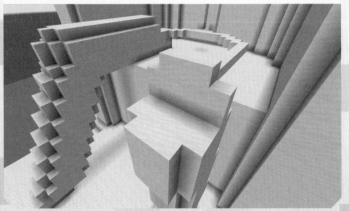

STEP 19

Make another frame like the one joining the hips to the highest part of the legs and build it up on the inner part of the legs.

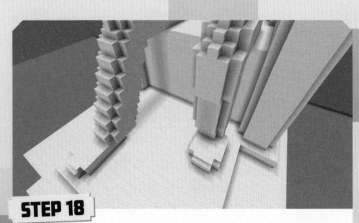

STEP 18

Fill in the open space using blocks to create a stepped pattern.

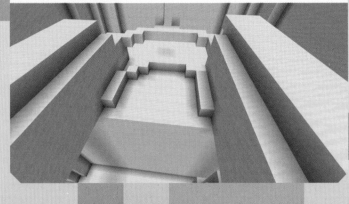

STEP 22

Build a frame for the torso like a rib cage, with the middle and bottom ribs coming to the front and the shoulders at the top starting further back. Add a support in the middle.

STEP 24

Start filling in the arms and hands, building up gradually.

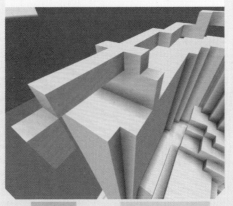

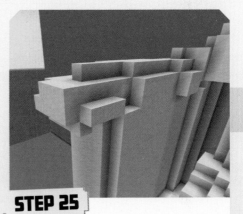

STEP 23

Fill in the rib cage to make the torso and add definition so it curves back.

STEP 25

Follow this image to build up the lines you have already created.

STEP 27

Build up the bottom of the face, making the chin jut out and adding to the cheeks.

STEP 26

Indent the bottom half of the face to define the shape.

STEP 28

Add ears, and use **smooth quartz stairs** for the nose and the ridge between the eyes.

STEP 29

Use upside-down **smooth quartz stairs** to create the top lip.

STEP 30

Use upside-down **smooth quartz stairs** for eyes as well and start to build up layers for the hair.

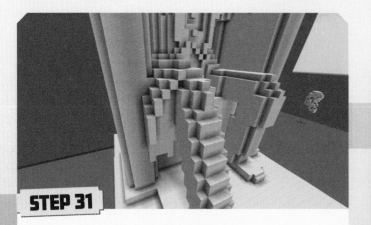

STEP 31

Add detail around the legs for the flag underneath the seated figure.

STEP 32

Add the flag draped behind the chair.

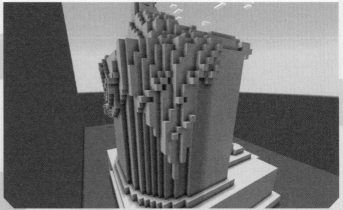

STEP 33

Fill out the back of the head in layers that get smaller as they go out so it has a deeper shape.

STEP 34

Use **smooth quartz stairs** and **smooth quartz slabs** to create the bow tie, and knock out the center of the torso to create an open jacket and shirt buttons.

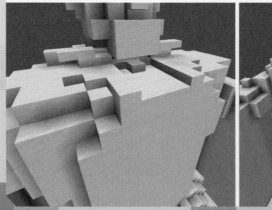

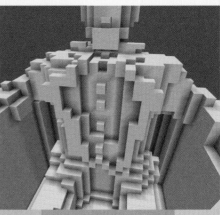

STEP 35

Add details to the back to create the draped look of the flag.

STEP 36

Check over your build and use **smooth quartz slabs** to smooth out any edges, adding more definition if you think it's needed.

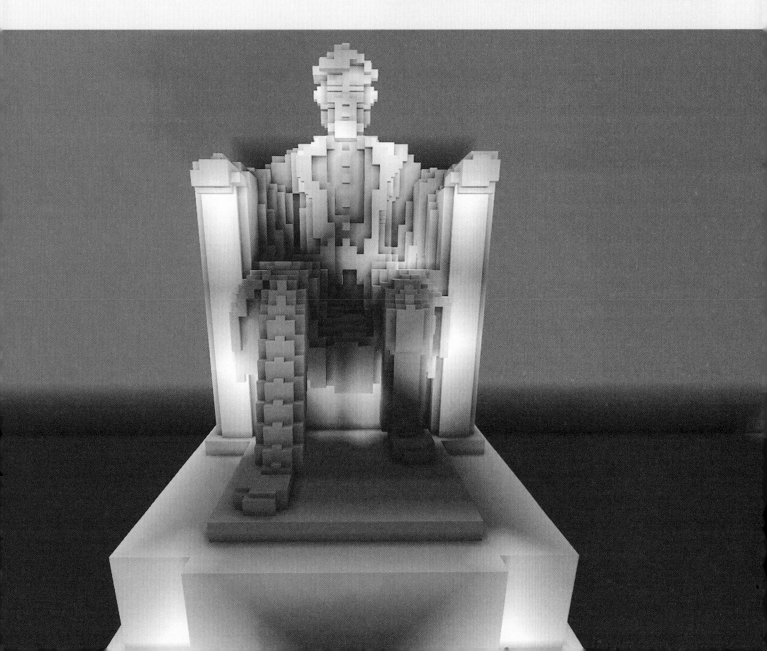

MARVELS OF ENGINEERING

Awesome constructions take some serious brain power and careful calculation before they can qualify as marvels of engineering.

SYDNEY OPERA HOUSE

The white roofs of Sydney Opera House, in Sydney, Australia, are arched to look like the sails of boats. Opened in 1973, its complex of theaters and halls is used for staging music, plays, and dance performances. More than 3,000 events take place in the Opera House every year.

The largest "sail" of the Opera House is as tall as a 20-story building.

BROOKLYN BRIDGE

The Brooklyn Bridge is a suspension bridge that goes across the East River from Brooklyn to Manhattan in New York City, USA. It was the first bridge to use steel for cable wire and was seen as a brilliant feat of 19th-century engineering. It was opened in 1883 and is an essential landmark of New York City!

DID YOU KNOW?

1,800 vehicles and 150,300 people crossed over the Brooklyn Bridge the day it opened. It was the only land passage between Manhattan and Brooklyn.

GOLDEN GATE BRIDGE

Connecting San Francisco to Marin County, the Golden Gate Bridge is 1.7 miles (2.7 km) long. It has six lanes for bicycles and pedestrians. When it was built, in 1937, it was the longest suspension bridge in the world. Around 40 million vehicles cross the bridge every year.

HOOVER DAM

Named in honor of the American president, Herbert Hoover, this dam was completed in under five years and finished in 1936. It is one of the largest concrete structures on Earth, weighing 6.6 million tons. It spans the Colorado River and holds back Lake Mead, providing hydroelectric power to Arizona, Nevada, and California.

Around seven million people visit the Eiffel Tower every year.

EIFFEL TOWER

Made of more than 18,000 separate parts, the Eiffel Tower in Paris, France, stands more than 1,050 feet (320 meters) tall. Started in 1889, it took 300 workers just under two years to build Gustave Eiffel's design.

MARVELS OF ENGINEERING

DIFFICULTY: EASY

BUILD TIME: 2+ HOURS

GOLDEN GATE BRIDGE

Are you ready to build one of the most recognizable bridges in the world? Tackling this will take serious calculation—and impressive building skills.

MATERIALS

- BLACK CONCRETE
- WHITE CONCRETE
- RED NETHER BRICK WALL
- MANGROVE FENCE
- RED CONCRETE
- LIGHT GRAY CONCRETE
- SMOOTH STONE

STEP 1

Find a stretch of water to build on. Use **black concrete** 7 blocks wide. Our bridge is 600 blocks long—make sure yours is an even number, too.

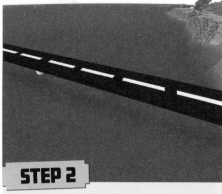

STEP 2

Run **white concrete** down the middle to create road markings.

STEP 3

Add a border of **light gray concrete**, 2 blocks wide, on both sides. Now add a row of **red nether brick wall**, 1 block wide, down each side.

STEP 4

Add **red concrete**, 1 block wide, down both sides and add **mangrove fence** along the top.

STEP 5

Use **red concrete**, 8 blocks deep, to fill in under your bridge.

STEP 6

Create the girder by knocking out these shapes from under your bridge. They are 3 blocks across and down.

STEP 7

Create the girder on the other side by repeating Step 5.

STEP 8

Use **red concrete** to create joints under the bridge.

STEP 9

Zoom out to check if it's looking ok. This is how it should look.

STEP 10

Start on the towers, using **red concrete**, around a fifth of the way along the bridge. Copy the shape below.

STEP 11

Build the tower up to around 50 blocks high. Repeat on the opposite side of the bridge.

STEP 12

Indent by 1 block and build up another 50 blocks. Make sure you do the same thing on the opposite side.

STEP 13

Keep building up and repeat twice more, but make these two slightly shorter, closer to 40 blocks high each.

STEP 14

Join the top of each set of blocks, indenting the center blocks. Copy the shape below.

STEP 15

Repeat the towers around a fifth of the way from the other end of your bridge.

STEP 16

Using **red concrete**, build steps down from the top of each tower to the end of your bridge. Each step is 2 blocks long and 1 block deep.

STEP 18

Build steps into the center from each tower. Make them 3 blocks wide, 1 block deep, and when you get to just above the middle, make them flat.

STEP 19

Use **mangrove fences** to create the wires over the middle of the bridge.

STEP 17

Under every other step, use **mangrove fences** to create the wires.

STEP 21

Where the beam meets the girder, build a layer of **red concrete**, a layer of **light gray concrete**, and another layer of **red concrete** around it.

STEP 20

Add **smooth stone** to the bottom of your towers.

STEP 22

Add **mangrove fencing** around the edge of the layers.

STEP 23

Add **mangrove fencing** up the side of the towers to look like ladders.

EIFFEL TOWER

One of the most famous towers in the world, and you're going to build it!
Can you reach its heights?

MATERIALS

- GRASS
- NETHERITE
- STONE
- IRON BARS
- ANDESITE WALL
- IRON TRAPDOORS

STEP 1

Using **grass** blocks as markers, create a square that is 31 x 31 blocks. Mark a cross down the center of your square. Use **stone** blocks in each corner to create a 7 x 7 square that is 2 blocks high.

STEP 3

At the very top, build a square that is 5 x 5 blocks with a cross in the middle.

STEP 4

Start to build up the legs, adding 2 blocks at a time going up from the far corners of the stone base to the corners of the first section.

STEP 2

Build upward for the tower from the centre—use **netherite** blocks and follow the measurements above.

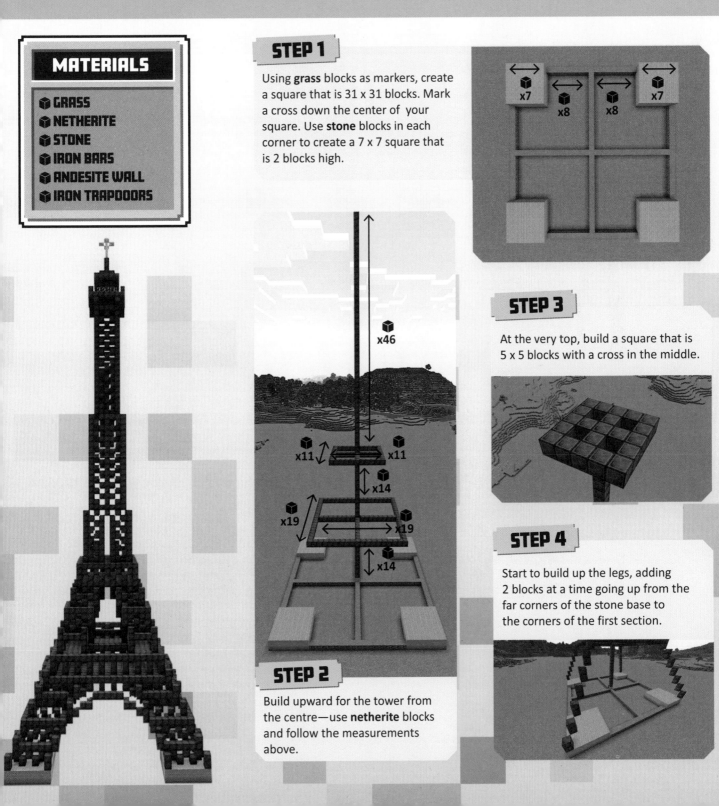

MARVELS OF ENGINEERING

DIFFICULTY: **INTERMEDIATE**

BUILD TIME: **4+ HOURS**

STEP 5

Build up the outer frame for the next level using the measurements above.

STEP 6

From the very top, build down 20 blocks from each corner. Then add another 11 blocks, out by 1 block. Build down 9 blocks, again out by 1 block.

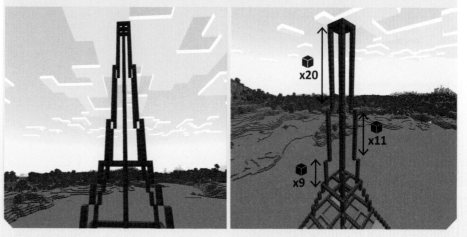

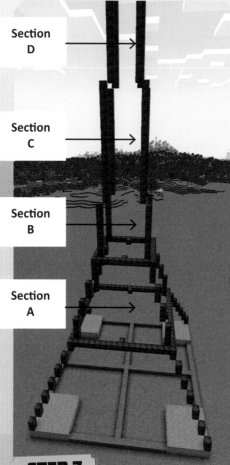

Section D

Section C

Section B

Section A

STEP 7

Knock out the central line of blocks going down the middle—it was just to help position the initial blocks.

STEP 8

Use the sections marked out in the previous step to help you. Go to the line of blocks between sections A and B, and build another square of blocks 2 blocks up into section B.

STEP 9

Start filling in section A, with 2 lines on each side going down in 3 blocks, then 3 blocks, then 4 blocks.

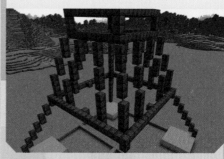

STEP 10

Under section A build another line of blocks around the whole tower—this should be 2 blocks down from the original frame.

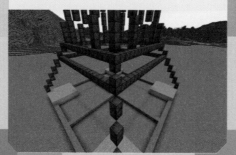

STEP 11

Make more legs by building on the outer corners of the stone bases. They will reach the bottom frame.

STEP 12

Repeat Step 11 and make more legs by building on the inner corners of the stone bases.

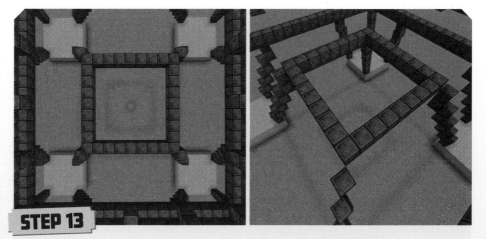

STEP 13

Now build a centre square where the legs from the inner corners meet.

STEP 14

Join the blocks on the legs, with lines across like below.

STEP 15

Fill in the gaps left on the legs using an alternating pattern.

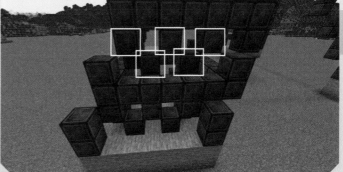

STEP 17

Build up a sort of cage shape from the center gap that is 3 blocks high.

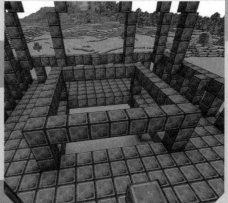

STEP 16

Fill in the space around the smaller square you built in the center. Once this is done, fill the space between the 2 levels using an alternating pattern.

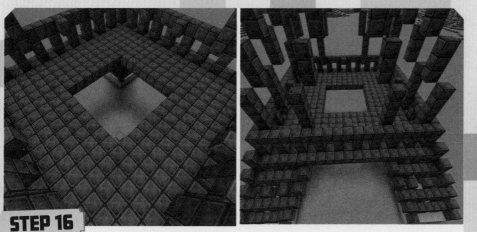

MARVELS OF ENGINEERING

STEP 18

From the cage shape, build up an arch like below. Then repeat on each side of the cage.

STEP 19

This is how section A of your tower should look at this stage.

STEP 20

Join the vertical lines horizontally so it starts to look filled in.

Make sure to do this all the way around.

STEP 22

Fill in the space between the two layers separating sections A and B in an alternating pattern.

STEP 21

It should look something like this.

STEP 23

Fill in section C as above, with a cross pattern down the center and 2 layers of alternating blocks down the edges.

STEP 24

Repeat this shape for section D but with only 1 layer of alternating blocks down the edges.

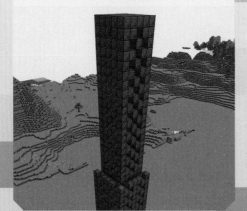

STEP 25

This is how your tower should look.

STEP 26

At the very top, add a platform, which overlaps by 1 block all around, and fill the spaces between the corners using **iron bars**.

STEP 27

In the center of your new platform, build a hut shape 4 blocks high and 3 x 3 wide.

STEP 28

Add a layer of blocks that overlaps and then a smaller layer on top of that. Add 3 blocks at the very top in the center and then a pile of 7 **andesite walls** on top of each other with 4 **iron trap doors** attached.

STEP 29

To finish off, create an arch between the legs of your tower.

To get to the top of the Eiffel Tower, you have to climb 1,665 steps. The fastest time anyone has climbed it in is seven minutes and 53 seconds.

DIFFICULTY: MASTER

BUILD TIME: 6+ HOURS

SYDNEY OPERA HOUSE

Can you make a build that's fit for the world's finest performers? Let's find out!

MATERIALS

- TERRACOTTA
- SAND
- SMOOTH SANDSTONE STAIRS
- WHITE CONCRETE
- BLACK STAINED GLASS PANE
- OXIDIZED CUT COPPER
- SANDSTONE WALL
- POLISHED DEEPSLATE WALL
- SEA LANTERN
- LEAVES

STEP 1

Use **terracotta** to make the below shape, using the measurements provided.

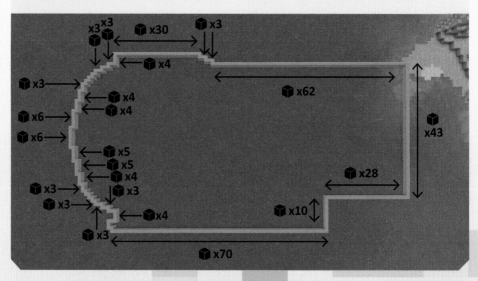

STEP 2

Fill in the shape so that it is 3 blocks deep. At the end, add 4 sets of **smooth sandstone stairs,** 56 blocks wide.

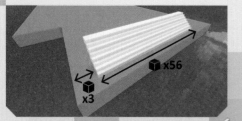

STEP 3

Build a platform using **sand.** Make it 20 blocks deep. Join it with the **terracotta** base with 4 more blocks.

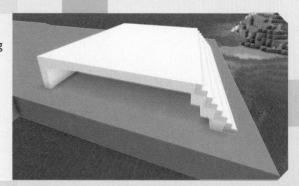

STEP 4

At the end of the platform that has a wider gap, build another smaller set of **smooth sandstone stairs** 13 blocks wide.

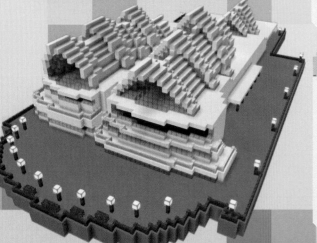

STEP 5

At the top of the smaller staircase, leave a 2-block space and then add a set of **smooth sandstone stairs,** then a row of **sand,** next another set of **smooth sandstone stairs.** They should be 24 blocks wide.

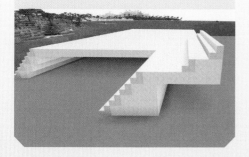

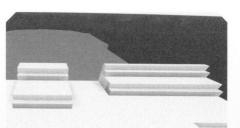

STEP 6

Leave a gap 4 blocks wide, then start on a new ledge. Repeat Step 5, but this time make the **sand** two blocks deep.

STEP 7

Continue your second ledge to the end. Build up a smaller wall in the gap with sand 2 blocks high.

STEP 8

From the ledges you have just built fill in 60 blocks deep going back.

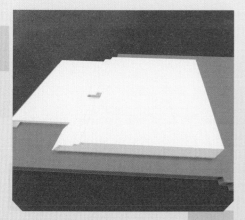

STEP 9

Use the measurements below to make the frame shape shown.

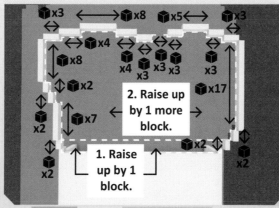

STEP 10

Join the frame shape to the **terracotta** base.

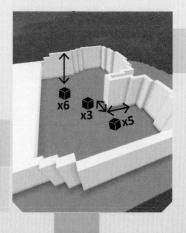

STEP 11

Fill in the top of your frame. Because you raised up layers in Step 9, you should now have 2 more ledges coming out of the platform from Step 8.

STEP 12

Use **smooth sandstone stairs** and **sand t**o build a set of stairs 4 blocks high along the front.

MARVELS OF ENGINEERING

STEP 13

Build back from the staircase you built in step 12 by 4 blocks and create the below ledge around the first curve.

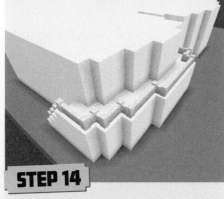

STEP 14

Add **sandstone wall** around the edge of the staircase and ledge.

STEP 15

Create this elaborate staircase using **smooth sandstone stairs**, **sandstone wall**, and **sand** on the other side of the front of the building.

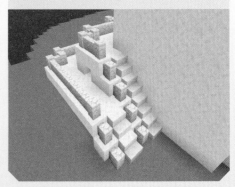

STEP 16

Add ledges all the way around the lower front edge and the upper front edge, and line it with **sandstone wall.**

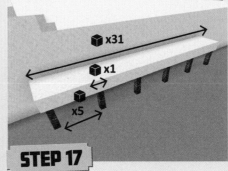

x31

x1

x5

STEP 17

At the side furthest away from the water, add this balcony using **sand** and two layers of **polished deepslate wall** as pillars.

STEP 18

Start to build 4 arches, indented in from the edge, using **white concrete**.

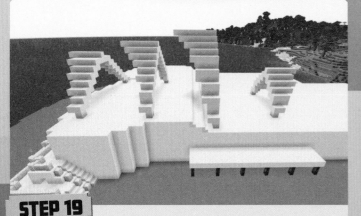

STEP 19

Fill out the arches, making them thicker toward the top.

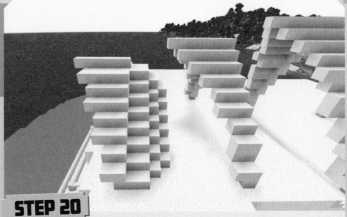

STEP 20

Add layers going back from the front arch.

STEP 22

Line the back of your third arch with **oxidized cut copper.**

STEP 21

Using the layering, join the front arch to the next one back.

STEP 24

This is how the join between your second and third arches should look.

STEP 23

Join the second and third arches.

STEP 26

Build up around the line at the back of your third arch.

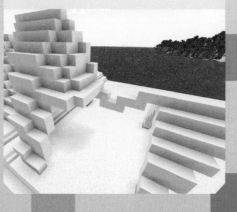

STEP 27

Fill in the gap between the last 2 arches (see below for detail).

STEP 25

Add this line between your third and fourth arches.

MARVELS OF ENGINEERING

STEP 28

This is how all the arches should look once you've joined them with layers.

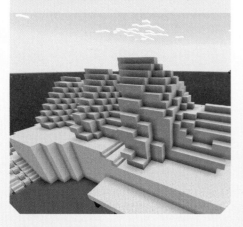

STEP 29

Fill both ends of the build with **black stained glass panes.**

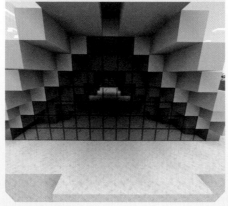

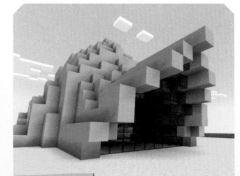

STEP 30

Add more layers of white concrete to the front top so that the center sticks out in layers.

STEP 31

Add more layers of **black stained glass panes** around the base of the front of your build.

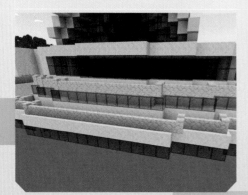

STEP 32

Now create 4 smaller arches that are to the side of the first set.

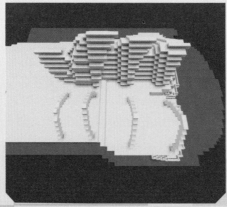

STEP 33

Thicken the new arches as you did in step 19.

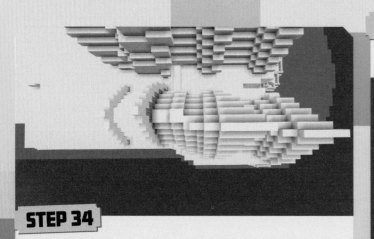

STEP 34

Fill in the gaps between your arches. Add a layer of **oxidized cut copper** at the front of your second arch.

STEP 35

Your 2 shapes should look like this from above.

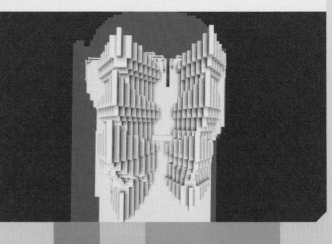

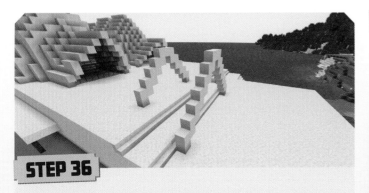

STEP 36

At the back of your first arched shape, build a few more arches that cross along the ledges you built in step 11. Line these ledges with **smooth sandstone** stairs to create a more defined edge.

STEP 37

Fill in these new arches as shown.

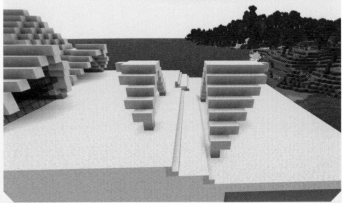

STEP 38

Fill in these new arches with **black stained glass panes** and extend the tops with **white concrete.**

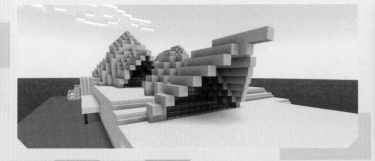

STEP 39

Add **polished deepslate wall, leaves,** and **sea lanterns** to finish off the front of your build.

CASTLES AND PALACES

Built for royalty, the rich, and the ruling classes, castles and palaces are normally grand buildings, with space to house many people, including servants.

MONT ST. MICHEL

The abbey of Mont St. Michel, in France, was built in the 8th century. It rests on an island that is cut off from the mainland by high tides. The structure reflects the social system of the time it was built, with the abbey at the top, and, at the bottom, the fishermen and farmers' houses. More than three million people visit every year.

SCHÖNBRUNN PALACE

A decorative 18th-century palace, near Vienna, Austria, with Baroque features, this was built to be fit for emperors. Used as an imperial summer residence, it features elaborate gardens that form part of the overall design of the palace.

DID YOU KNOW?

Schönbrunn means "beautiful spring". It's named after the well from where the court got its water.

TOWER OF LONDON

In the 1070s, William the Conqueror began to build a massive stone fortress in London to defend and proclaim his royal power. The tower took around 20 years to build. Throughout history, the tower has been adapted and developed with more walls, towers, and a moat.

MATSUE CASTLE

Matsue, in Japan, is known as the "city of water" and the castle is surrounded by moats. It was built in 1611, and the main keep has survived fires and other natural disasters through the years. Its design is like the shape of a bird's spread-out wings

NEUSCHWANSTEIN CASTLE

This elaborate, romantic castle was built at a time when castles were no longer needed as strongholds. King Louis II of Bavaria, Germany, ordered its construction during 1868, but it was never fully completed. Although medieval in design, King Louis also wanted it to be as modern as possible.

It was the inspiration for Disneyland's Sleeping Beauty Castle.

TOWER OF LONDON

Can you construct your own Tower of London? There is everything here to help you through it—just don't get locked in the tower!

MATERIALS

- SANDSTONE BLOCKS
- QUARTZ BRICKS
- QUARTZ SLABS
- QUARTZ STAIRS
- OXIDIZED COPPER
- CYAN TERRACOTTA
- BIRCH FENCE
- SANDSTONE WALL
- IRON WALL
- DARK OAK FENCE
- DARK OAK SLABS
- DARK OAK BLOCKS
- DRAGON HEAD

STEP 1

Create a frame for your build. Make 2 squares for the corner towers, 1 circle for the circle tower, and a large curve in one corner. Steps 2 and 3 will explain how to make the circle and curve shapes. The frame has been laid out so you can see the pattern between the main **sandstone blocks** and the **quartz blocks** that form the accents along the walls.

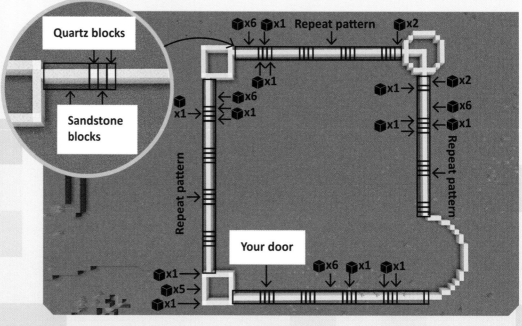

Quartz blocks

Sandstone blocks

x6 x1 Repeat pattern x2

x1

x1 x6 x1

x2 x1 x6 x1

Repeat pattern

Your door

x1 x5 x1 x6 x1 x1

This building is the most famous part of the Tower of London—known as the "White Tower."

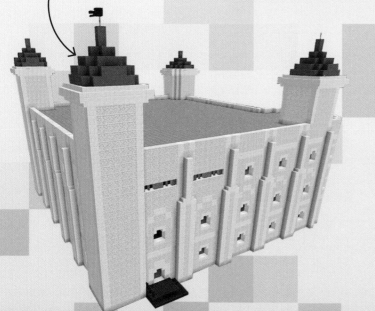

STEP 2

Create the circle tower using the measurements below.

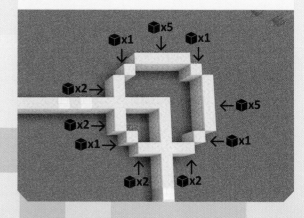

x5 x1 x1

x2 x5

x2 x1

x2 x2

STEP 3

Now use these measurements to create the curved corner.

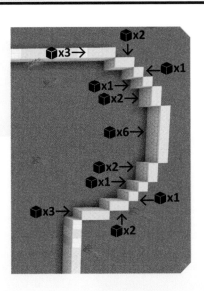

Add lines of Quartz bricks as decoration along your walls.

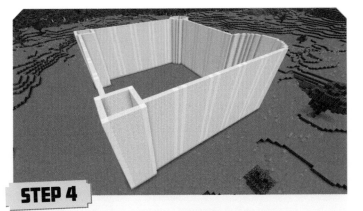

STEP 4

Build up 22 blocks high on all sides from your frame.

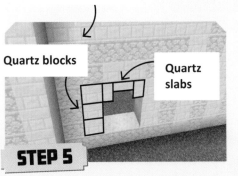

Quartz blocks

Quartz slabs

STEP 5

Create a door where it's marked out in Step 1. Knock out a space of 4 blocks wide and 3 blocks high. Then knock out 2 blocks above that in the center of the door. Fill the edges with **quartz bricks** and **quartz slabs** at the top to create a decorative top.

STEP 6

Above the door, add a window by knocking out a space 2 blocks wide and 3 blocks high. Fill the bottom of the window with 2 **quartz blocks** and the top with **quartz slabs**.

Add quartz block arches.

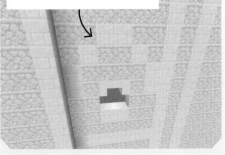

STEP 7

Above the window, add another longer window. Do this by knocking out a space of 6 blocks. Fill this space with **sandstone wall** and **birch fence**. Repeat this step on the right side as well.

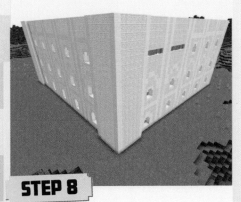

STEP 8

Add windows all the way around your build, but don't add them to your towers.

STEP 9

Add windows across the curved corner.

STEP 10

Use **dark oak fences, dark oak blocks**, and **dark oak slabs** to create a small staircase outside the door.

STEP 11

Add extra blocks around the edges of your build. They need to match your pattern and will stick out to add definition. At the top, add a line of **quartz blocks** in the center.

STEP 12

Fill in your roof using **oxidized copper**, but do not fill the towers.

STEP 13

Build up your towers so they are 7 blocks high.

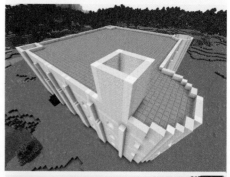

STEP 14

Surround the tops of your towers with **quartz stairs.** Fill in the bottom with **cyan terracotta** and add a line of blocks in the middle, 5 blocks high.

STEP 15

Using **cyan terracotta**, fill in your tower spires.

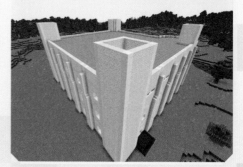

STEP 16

Add an iron fence with a **dragon head** on the top of each of your towers.

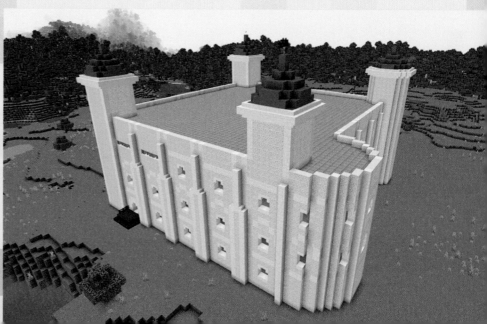

MATSUE CASTLE

Built on the edge of water, Matsue Castle will truly test the depths of your ability. But be careful not to don't fall in!

MATERIALS

- POLISHED BLACKSTONE BRICK
- POLISHED BLACKSTONE BRICK STAIRS
- STONE
- STONE STAIRS
- WHITE CONCRETE
- DARK OAK WOOD
- DARK OAK FENCE
- BLACK STAINED GLASS PANE
- MANGROVE PLANKS
- MANGROVE FENCE
- MANGROVE DOOR
- ACACIA TRAPDOOR

STEP 1

Start by building a square using **stone** that is 41 blocks x 41 blocks.

STEP 2

Add 4 diagonal blocks stepping up in each corner.

STEP 3

Build stepped lines of blocks using step 2 as a guide.

STEP 4

Fill in the top of this base using **stone**.

STEP 5

Make this shape using seven **dark oak wood** blocks and then indent for 5 blocks, then repeat, until you have the shape above.

STEP 6

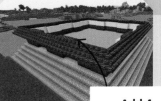

On top of your **dark oak wood** shape, add 3 layers of **polished blackstone brick stairs**. Step them out so they hang over the edge.

Add 4 polished blackstone brick blocks in the indents.

The dark color of the wood is due to a dye made from unripe persimmons left stewing for five years.

CASTLES AND PALACES

STEP 8

For the next layer, add 2 more layers of **dark oak wood** followed by a layer of **white concrete**.

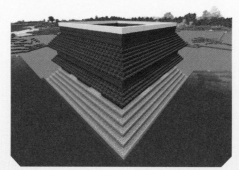

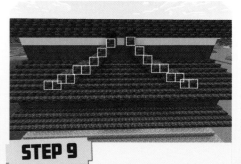

STEP 7

Add 2 more layers of **dark oak wood** followed by a layer of **white concrete**. On top of that, add 4 more layers of **polished blackstone brick stairs,** stepping them out over the edge again.

STEP 9

Add 2 layers of **polished blackstone brick stairs** and then **polished blackstone brick** blocks into an peaked shape as above.

STEP 11

Put 4 more layers of **polished blackstone brick stairs** on top of the stairs you added in step 9. Then add 2 layers of **dark oak wood** followed by a layer of **white concrete**. Finish it off with 6 more layers of **polished blackstone brick stairs**.

This is the back view.

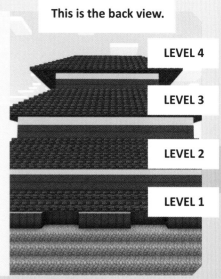

LEVEL 4

LEVEL 3

LEVEL 2

LEVEL 1

STEP 10

Add a layer of white concrete inside the tent shape you just created and fill with **black stained glass panes**. Add 2 extra blocks of **white concrete** in the top center with 1 block of **dark oak wood** below. Add a windowsill of **dark oak wood** along the bottom, the full width of the window frame.

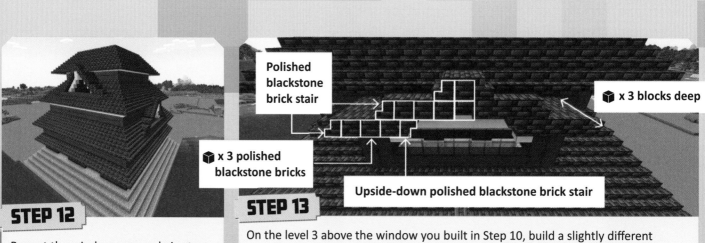

Polished blackstone brick stair

x 3 blocks deep

x 3 polished blackstone bricks

Upside-down polished blackstone brick stair

STEP 12

Repeat the window you made in step 10 on level 3 to the left side of the first window.

STEP 13

On the level 3 above the window you built in Step 10, build a slightly different window. Use blocks of **dark oak wood** in a line with 3 blocks high for the 2 end blocks. Add 2 layers of **black stained glass panes**. Add **polished blackstone brick stairs** and **polished blackstone brick** blocks as above.

STEP 14

Using **polished blackstone brick** blocks, build a tent shape at both ends of your roof 5 blocks high. The first 2 sets should be 2 blocks wide, then change the last 2 to 1 block with 1 in the middle.

STEP 15

Fill in the sides of the roof using **polished blackstone brick stairs**. Use **black stained glass panes** and **white concrete** at the front and back ends to let light in.

STEP 16

Go back to the stone base you built in Step 4 and use **stone stairs** along all of the edges you created. This will create the look of steeper and more detailed stairs.

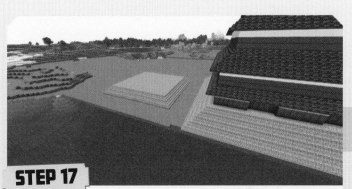

STEP 17

At a distance of about 6 blocks away, build a square that is 28 x 28 blocks. Use **stone** and **stone stairs** to create a base that is 3 blocks high (it will look like 6 because of the **stone stairs** around the edges).

STEP 18

Now add 2 layers of **dark oak wood**, 1 layer of **white concrete**, and 2 layers of **polished blackstone brick stairs**. Repeat with 2 layers of **dark oak wood**, 1 layer of **white concrete**, and then add 4 layers of **polished blackstone brick stairs**.

STEP 19

Along the middle of the new building, add a line of **polished blackstone brick** to connect the two buildings.

STEP 20

Use 6 sets of **polished blackstone brick stairs** to make the connecting line more defined.

STEP 21

Below the connecting line of stairs, add 2 layers of **dark oak wood,** then 2 layers of **polished blackstone brick stairs**. Add a layer of **white concrete** and 2 more layers of **dark oak wood**. finish off with more **stone stairs**.

STEP 22

On top on the smaller building, add a peaked frame for the roof at each end. Then fill in the sides of the roof using **polished blackstone brick stairs.**

STEP 23

Now make a window as you did in step 15 for this roof.

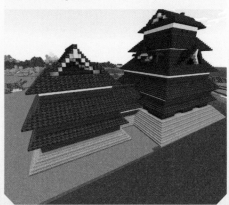

STEP 24

On the other side of your bigger building, add 2 layers of **polished blackstone brick stairs that intersect** with the current second level. This should be 15 x 15 blocks.

STEP 25

Add 4 more layers of **polished black-stone brick stairs** down the sides. Make smaller windows with 1 layer of **dark oak wood**, 1 layer of **black stained glass panes**, and 1 single **white concrete** block in the center.

STEP 26

Build down with a layer of **white concrete blocks** that should line up with the bigger building. Below that line up 2 layers of **dark oak wood** and 2 layers of **polished blackstone brick stairs**.

STEP 27

Below what you've just built, add 2 15 x 31 block layers of **polished blackstone brick stairs.**

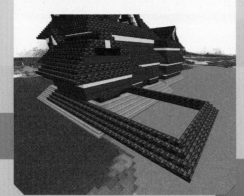

STEP 28

Under this add a layer of **white concrete** and 2 layers of **dark oak wood.**

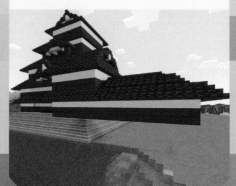

STEP 29

Add another layer of **white concrete** below, and at the far end, build down by another 4 blocks to touch the ground.

STEP 31

Fill the gap with **dark oak wood**.

STEP 30

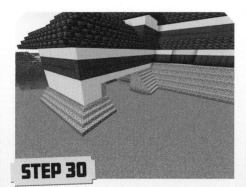

Add more layers of **stone stairs** so that they are in line with the **stone stairs** that are already surrounding the build, leaving a gap as above.

STEP 32

Make sure the rest of your building has an even amount of **stone stairs.**

STEP 33

Around the part of the building you built in Step 29, add an edge of **mangrove planks** 2 blocks wide and 1 block deep. Surround it with **mangrove fencing** and some **mangrove doors**.

STEP 34

Knock out some pieces for windows along the building. You can use **acacia trapdoors** for smaller windows and **dark oak fences** over **white concrete** with glass panes for a more classic window look.

Plant some cherry blossom trees around your castle to give it a more authentic Japanese feel.

CASTLES AND PALACES

DIFFICULTY:
MASTER

BUILD TIME:
6+ HOURS

SCHÖNBRUNN PALACE

This beautiful Baroque palace represents a royal challenge.
Can you match the aristocrats at their own game? Let's get started!

MATERIALS

- SANDSTONE
- QUARTZ
- QUARTZ STAIRS
- BONE
- SMOOTH SANDSTONE
- GRAY STAINED GLASS PANES
- BLUE STAINED GLASS BLOCKS
- DARK OAK DOORS
- RED NETHER BRICK STAIRS
- DARK OAK PLANKS
- NETHER PLANKS
- CUT SANDSTONE SLABS
- CUT SANDSTONE
- IRON BARS
- ANDESITE WALL
- SMOOTH STONE
- DEEPSLATE STAIRS
- GOLD

STEP 1

Start by laying out the base shape with **sandstone** blocks. Use the dimensions below.

x32 · x10 · x14 · x22 · x34 · x4 · x15 · x2 · x1 · x4 · x3 · x2 · x10 · x20 · x26 · x6 · x16 · x16 · x4 · x16

This build is symmetrical, so use the same measurements on both sides.

STEP 2

On the left at the front, knock out 2 blocks of sandstone and build up by 4 blocks. Then build over the top to make a bridge. Layer up using the materials below.

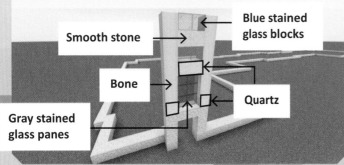

Smooth stone

Blue stained glass blocks

Bone

Quartz

Gray stained glass panes

STEP 3

Continue layering along the full 16 blocks of space, using the measurements below. The quartz is marked to help you.

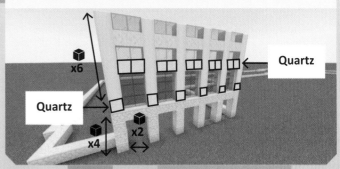

Quartz

x6

Quartz

x4

x2

STEP 4

Repeat Steps 2-3 for the next wall, but keep a layer of **sandstone** across the bottom and fill the remaining 2-block space with **blue stained glass blocks**.

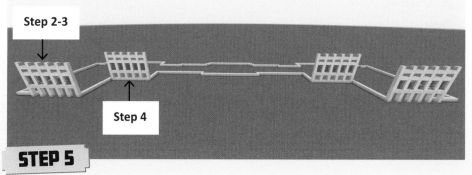

Step 2-3

Step 4

STEP 5

Repeat Steps 2-4 on the right-hand side of your build.

STEP 6

Use the same layering technique to fill in the walls that join the ones already built.

STEP 7

Use the same layering for the 20 block spaces at the front and for the joining wall next to it.

STEP 8

Fill in the back 32-block space using the same layering but use 6 blocks of alternating **bone** and **sandstone** stripes near the center, leaving 2 blocks clear. Do this on both sides.

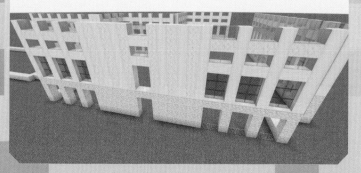

STEP 9

Fill in the back corners of the build like above.

CASTLES AND PALACES

STEP 10

Fill in the rest of the build, except for the 26-block space in the middle of the front, using the layering method from Step 4. Add sets of 2 **dark oak door**s along the back and front as marked in the image below and repeat on the right-hand side.

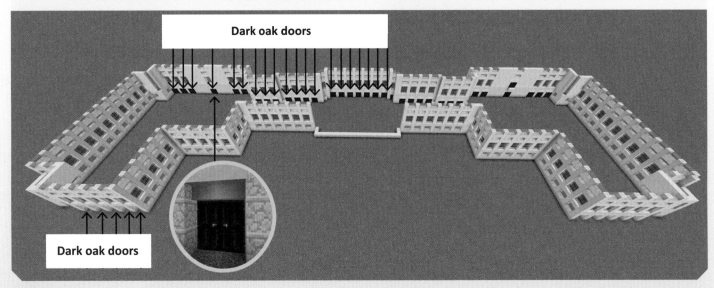

Dark oak doors

Dark oak doors

STEP 11

Now build the front entrance. From left to right: 2 **sandstone blocks**, 2 **dark oak doors**, 1 **sandstone block**, 1 **quartz block**, 2 **blue stained glass blocks**, 1 **quartz block**, 3 **sandstone blocks**, 2 **dark oak doors** and repeat.

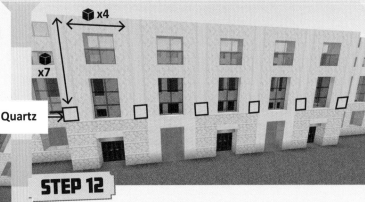

Quartz

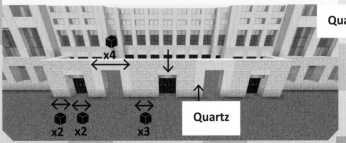

Quartz

STEP 12

Build up the front, with **sandstone blocks, gray stained glass panes, blue stained glass blocks, bone,** and **quartz blocks** mirroring the rest of the build, but seal off the top.

STEP 13

Add a layer of **quartz blocks** all around the outside edge of the build.

STEP 14

Add a layer of **cut sandstone slabs** across the top of the rest of the build.

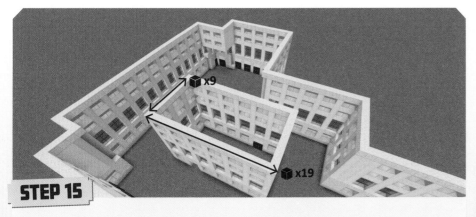

STEP 15

Build a smaller room inside the left-hand corner of your palace. It should mirror the outside design with **sandstone blocks**, **gray stained glass panes**, **blue stained glass blocks**, **bone**, and **quartz blocks.**

STEP 16

Use **red nether brick stairs** for your roof. Build up 6 layers around the top of the left-hand section. You should be left with 2 rectangular empty spaces at the top.

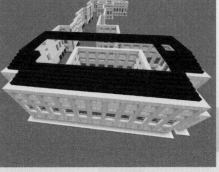

STEP 17

Keep adding to the roof until the room from Step 15 has brick stairs at the edge of its walls above it. Use **nether plank** blocks to fill the other empty space.

STEP 18

Build a small room, like in step 15, on the right-hand side of your build, but make it horizontal. Use **red nether brick stairs** for the roof, leaving some space to fill with **nether plank blocks** as below. Leave one small rectangle space at the front of the build, as shown.

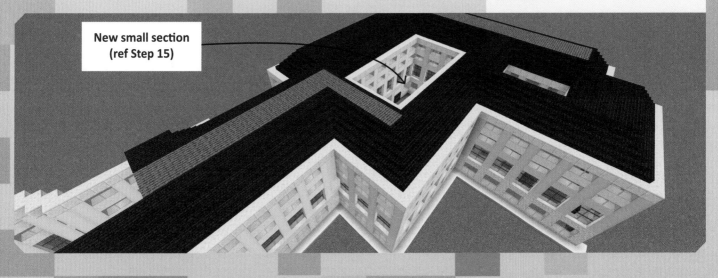

New small section (ref Step 15)

CASTLES AND PALACES

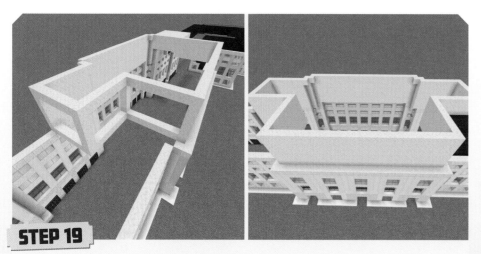

STEP 19

At the front, build up a frame in the center 6 blocks high, following the shape above, using **smooth sandstone**.

STEP 20

Decorate the front with stripes of **cut sandstone** and **quartz** blocks at the bottom. For the windows, use 2 **blue stained glass blocks** with 1 block of **dark oak planks** above them.

Cut sandstone

Dark oak planks

STEP 21

Use the image below to help fill in the rest of the roof.

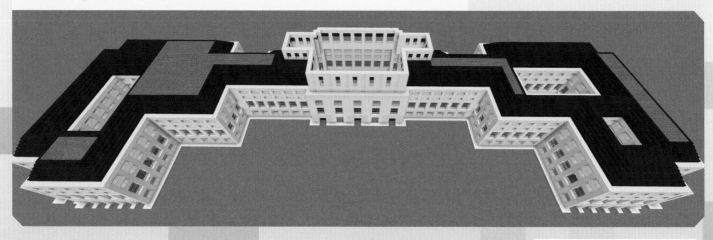

STEP 22

Add 2 blocks of **iron bars** around the top edges of the roof. In between, add **smooth stone** with **andesite wall** on the top.

Add layered nether plank blocks to these corners.

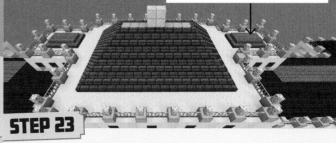

STEP 23

At the front and center of the palace, add a layer of **deepslate stairs**. Make them 5 blocks high, 17 blocks wide at the bottom and 8 at the top. Use **smooth stone** along the middle, with 4 blocks of **gold** at the very top.

STEP 24

Use **quartz stairs**, **quartz blocks**, and **iron bars** to create a staircase and balcony across the front of the palace. This should be 34 blocks wide. Use 4 layers of **andesite wall** as pillars for your balcony.

STEP 25

Create similar balconies on the left and right of your build, but they do not need stairs.

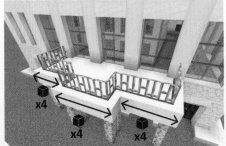

STEP 26

Add a number of chimneys using **smooth stone** with **andesite wall** on top—they can be placed wherever you like.

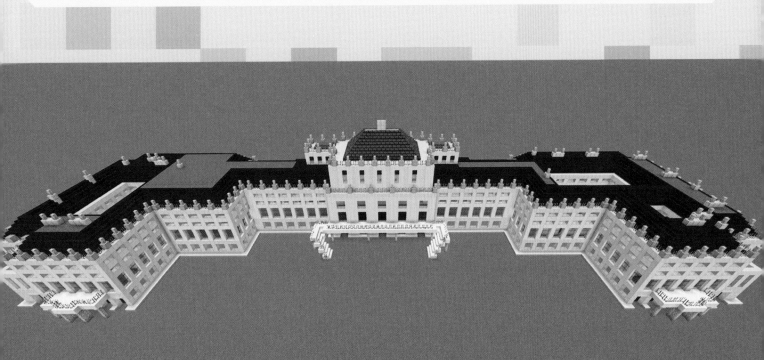

TAJ MAHAL

An example of perfect symmetry, this wonder of the world will push your skills to the limit!

DID YOU KNOW?

The Taj Mahal took 20,000 people more than 20 years to complete. It was started in 1632.

The Taj Mahal looks the same from all sides—it's perfectly symmetrical! It was built by the Mughal emperor Shah Jahan in the 17th century, as a tribute to his favorite wife, Mumtaz Mahal, after her death. The name means "crown of palaces," and 43 varieties of precious and semi-precious stones were used to decorate the tomb. It is situated on the banks of the River Yamuna in Agra, in Northern India.

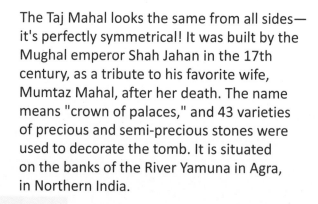

White marble

MATERIALS

- **BLOCK OF QUARTZ**
- **CHISELED QUARTZ BLOCK**
- **QUARTZ BRICKS**
- **QUARTZ STAIRS**
- **ANDESITE WALL**
- **IRON DOOR**
- **NETHER QUARTZ PILLAR**

STEP 1

Make a big square using **blocks of quartz**—it needs to be 101 x 101.

STEP 2

Make the square 3 blocks deep, and around each corner, make a circle shape. (Use the circle guide reference on page 80.)

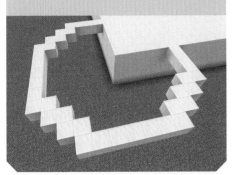

STEP 3

Fill in the circles—make sure you fill in 3 blocks down so they reach the ground.

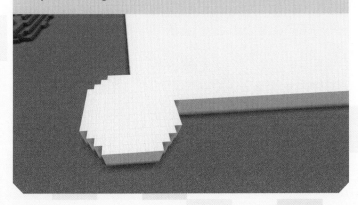

STEP 4

Around the top edge of your build, add a ridge of **andesite wall**.

STEP 5

At the front in the center, build a rectangle that is 6 x 21 blocks and 3 blocks high. Leave a 2-block-wide gap at each end, like a door.

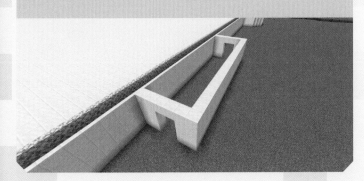

STEP 6

In the middle of this rectangle, build a 5 x 5 square. Run **andesite wall** around the edge, but open it up where the 5 x 5 square is.

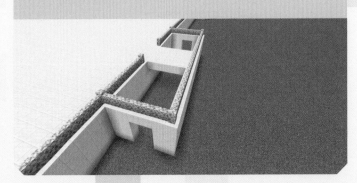

CASTLES AND PALACES

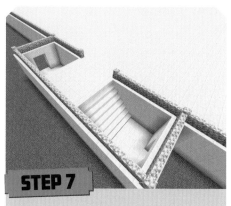

STEP 7

Add a floor at the bottom, and **quartz stairs,** on each side, coming up to meet at the square you just built.

STEP 8

Add a big cross shape in the center of the build. Each line should be 33 blocks long, and there should be a gap where they meet at the center.

STEP 9

Make a square around the cross, but round off the corners, and then mark points for the corners.

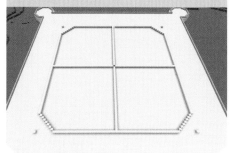

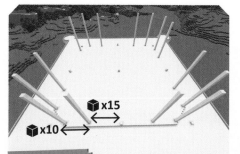

STEP 10

At each end of the rounded corners, build up 25 blocks of **chiseled quartz** pillars and repeat 15 blocks from your center marker.

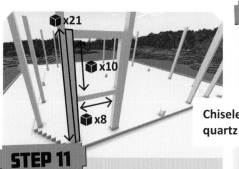

STEP 11

On the front left of the build, take the first 2 pillars and join them together by laying **blocks of quartz** according to the measurements above.

STEP 12

Add to the top and bottom with a layer of **quartz bricks.**

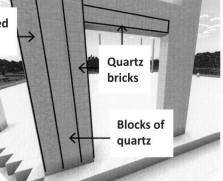

Chiseled quartz →

Quartz bricks

Blocks of quartz

STEP 13

Using **quartz bricks**, create an indent by building back by 4 blocks and then make a layer 2 blocks high.

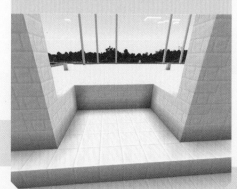

STEP 14

Make a wall at the back using **blocks of quartz.** Use **chiseled quartz** to decorate the front.

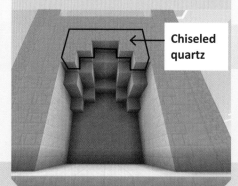

Chiseled quartz

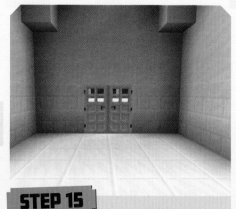

STEP 15

At the front, add in **2 iron doors** to the center.

STEP 16

Repeat the steps you just used to create the wall and doors to build them again so it's duplicated upward.

STEP 17

Now build the same structure on the other side of the front of the building. Use **blocks of quartz** to build a frame joining the structures.

STEP 18

Fill in the frame with 3 rows of **chiseled quartz**.

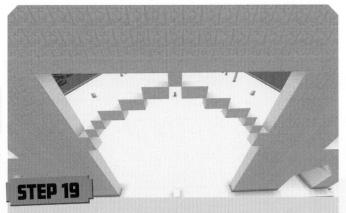

STEP 19

Build an arch shape at the top of the frame, like the above, across the center.

STEP 20

Fill in the arch shape with **chiseled quartz**. Build back from the arch by 7 blocks. The bottom 2 layers should be **quartz bricks**, and the rest should be **blocks of quartz**.

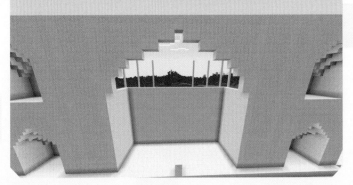

STEP 21

Build an elaborate layered roof using **blocks of quartz** and **quartz stairs.**

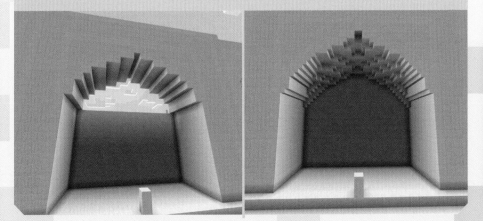

STEP 22

In the center, add 3 **iron doors** and decorate around them using **chiseled quartz**.

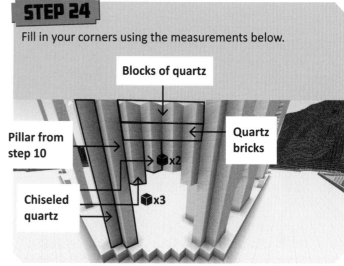

STEP 24

Fill in your corners using the measurements below.

Blocks of quartz

Quartz bricks

Pillar from step 10

×2

Chiseled quartz

×3

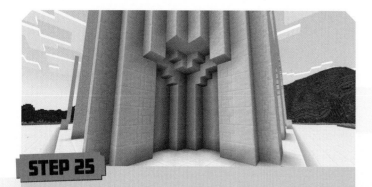

STEP 23

This is how the front of the build should look.

STEP 26

Repeat Step 25 so you duplicate upward. It should look like the below image.

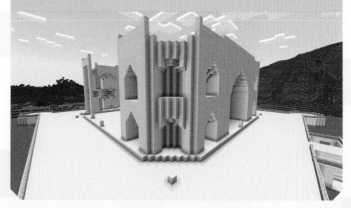

STEP 25

Fill in the gaps in the corners, using the above image as a guide. Upside-down **quartz stairs** have been included to create a more layered and detailed look.

STEP 27

Repeat the build on all sides and corners so it is symmetrical. Line up the corners with the top of the build. Fill in the top of the build with **blocks of quartz.**

STEP 28

Run **andesite wall** around the top edges of the build. Now add 5-block-high pillars in the same places that you put them in Step 10. Use upside-down **quartz stairs** in a square formation to create a ledge at the top of each pillar. Add a **block of quartz** in the middle and a block of **andesite wall** on top of that.

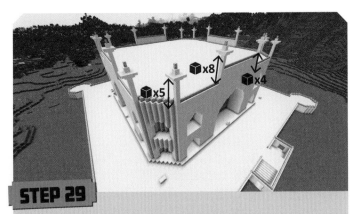

STEP 29

Once you have completed all the pillars, raise the front and back parts of your build slightly to make them taller than the rest.

STEP 30

On top of the build, 3 blocks in from the corners, use **chiseled quartz** to create these circles.

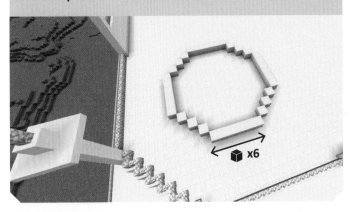

STEP 31

Build a frame around your circles with **blocks of quartz** 3 blocks high. Mark where the center of the roof will go in the middle of the main build.

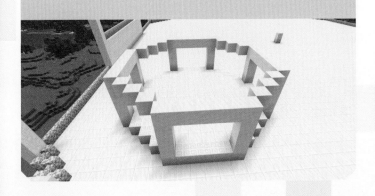

STEP 32

Make a dome by adding a layered roof with **blocks of quartz** and **quartz stairs**. Leave openings at the sides to look like doors and leave the corners open.

STEP 33

Repeat the domes in each corner of the build. It should now look like this.

STEP 34

On top of all your domes add 4 blocks of **nether quartz pillars**, and then add a 4-block-wide **andesite wall** that is also 4 blocks high.

CASTLES AND PALACES

STEP 35

Use the center mark you made to lay out a cross in **blocks of quartz,** 15 x 15 blocks.

STEP 36

Make a circle around this cross, and build up walls that are 6 blocks high. Across the top, build an arch, but leave a 7-block gap in the middle.

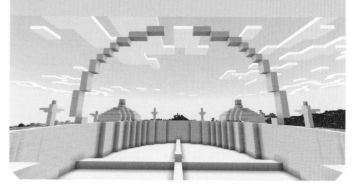

STEP 37

Build more arches, but keep leaving a 7-block gap. Then build a circle in the center that the gap has left.

STEP 38

Fill the central dome using the arches you have just created as a frame.

STEP 39

At the top, layer the blocks as above.

STEP 40

Go back to the circles you made in steps 2-4. Build an indented circle, and then add a cross on top using **blocks of quartz.**

STEP 41

Build up from the indented circle and cross to make a tower 36 blocks high.

STEP 42

Create some shapes at the top to round off your tower.

STEP 43

Use upside-down **quartz stairs** to split your towers into thirds. Now repeat steps 41-44 to make the other towers.

Use andesite wall to create a decorative finish

CIRCLE GUIDE

To keep things simple, all building materials in Minecraft have blocky right angles. But there are ways of putting these boxy shapes together to create something like a curve. This is a perfect example of how blocks don't necessarily have to be used in the way they were intended: steps and tiles can be cleverly placed to create edges that are different from the standard block.

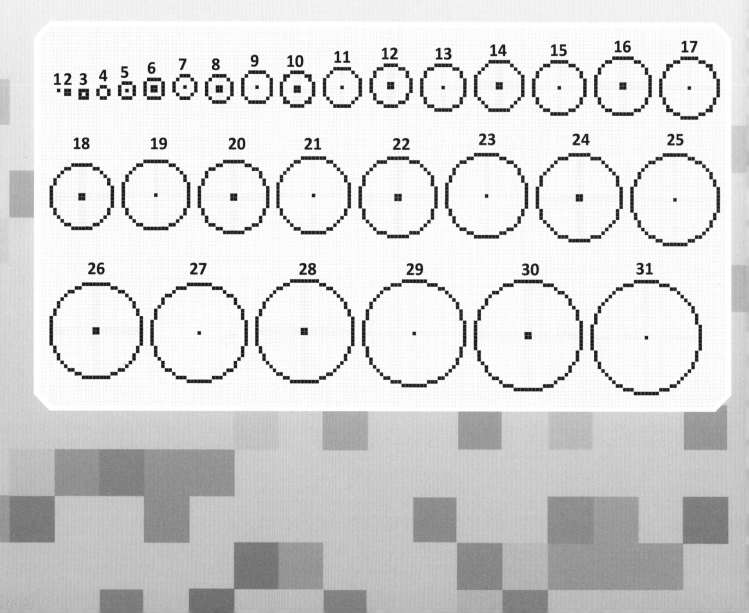